Mind
Sell

THE BEST *LITTLE* SALES BOOK *EVER*

Mind
Sell

Chris Helder

Published in 2025 by Dean Publishing

DEAN PUBLISHING

PO Box 119
Mt. Macedon, Victoria, 3441
Australia
deanpublishing.com
Copyright © 2025 Chris Helder
Cataloguing-in-Publication Data
National Library of Australia
Title: Mindsell: the best little sales book ever
ISBN: 978-0-64899-571-5

CONTENTS

INTRODUCTION TO MINDSELL

SELLING TODAY (WHAT HAS CHANGED?)

Some people insist that the fundamentals of selling haven't changed. They say success still comes down to building rapport, asking great questions, connecting with people, and delivering value. Others argue that technology has flipped the sales world on its head, making traditional methods less important. The truth is, both sides are right.

Technology, especially artificial intelligence, automation, and data-driven insights, has completely revolutionised the landscape. We can now research clients in minutes, segment prospects with laser precision, and engage entire markets with a click of a button. CRM (customer relationship management) systems predict buying windows. AI drafts emails before we even finish our morning coffee. Selling has become faster, sharper, and more efficient than ever before.

But here's the kicker: technology doesn't close deals. People do.

That fact remains as true today as it ever was. While technology can open a door, all the tech in the world can't walk through it for you. It can't read hesitation in a voice, pick up excitement in a client's body language, or navigate the emotional currents that run through every meaningful sale. Once the appointment is booked or the first call connects, the human element takes over. And that's where the real magic happens.

This is the beating heart of *MindSell*. This book is about mastering the space where science meets strategy. The tools get you into the room, but you, with presence, insight, and influence, win the trust and the business. It's about showing up in those critical moments with something technology can't replicate: authenticity, empathy, and leadership.

THE INTERSECTION OF INFLUENCE AND SELLING

Understanding simple principles of influence in sales isn't about slick manipulation. It's about deep awareness and seeing the world through your clients' eyes, understanding how people think, decide, act, and buy. It's about knowing the emotional forces that drive human behaviour, and then aligning your communication with those forces rather than pushing against them.

One of my favourite insights into selling is, "People don't buy from the best salesperson, they buy from the one who understands them best." That's the key. It's not about being the flashiest or loudest. It's about being *aligned*.

Today's most successful sales professionals aren't just experts in their products. They're students of behaviour. They know how to create trust faster, how to defuse tension when it arises, and how to guide decisions with subtlety and strength. They understand that selling is no longer just a numbers game, but also a neuroscience game.

To succeed in today's environment, you must master two intertwined forces: the smart use of technology and the timeless power of human-to-human influence.

Most organisations have embraced the tech revolution. CRM platforms, predictive analytics, and AI-driven marketing are all designed to scale outreach, optimise timing, and automate the basics. These systems are vital. They open doors faster. They multiply touchpoints. But they don't close the deal. They don't build rapport in a meeting, earn trust during a tough conversation, or sense when a client is hesitating beneath their words. Only a skilled human can do that.

And that's why human-to-human influence has never been more valuable. When you're face-to-face with a client, whether in person, over a virtual platform, or even on a simple phone call, your ability to read, respond, and lead emotionally is the true separator. It's not about who can talk the most or who has the most polished offering. It's about who can connect fastest, understand deepest, and build the strongest bridge between need and solution.

Customers today are savvier than ever. They've researched your product, read the reviews, checked out your competitors, and probably trawled your LinkedIn profile before they meet you. They're flooded with information. And ironically, that flood doesn't make decision-making easier; it makes it harder.

In fact, a recent Gartner study found that 77 percent of B2B buyers described their last buying experience as "extremely complex or difficult." This wasn't because they lacked information, but because they had *too much information.*[1] Nowadays, buyers aren't just looking for a better product. They're looking for clarity. They're looking for someone they trust to help them filter through the noise.

If you can't be that trusted guide, you'll find yourself competing on price. And competing on price is a dangerous race to the bottom, because as the old saying goes: "In the absence of value, people buy on price." And someone will always be willing to go lower. You don't want to play that game. You want to be the person they trust, not the one they price-shop.

In this book, I'll show you how to understand and influence people. It's not about manipulation, but rather how to lead. I'll show you the steps to create deeper emotional connections faster, how to guide decisions with integrity and turn every conversation into an opportunity to build trust and momentum.

Because selling today isn't about slick pitches or clever closing tricks. It's about understanding how people think, what they need, and how they decide. Then leading from connection, not pressure. It's about becoming not just someone your customers want to buy from, but someone they're *relieved* to buy from.

MindSell isn't about working harder. It's about working *deeper*. It's about selling in a way that feels energizing, fulfilling, and sustainable, not exhausting and transactional. Because when you master the intersection of influence and selling, you don't just win deals; you build a career, a reputation, and a life you can be proud of.

ENTER THE MINDSELL MODEL

In a world flooded with sales advice, gimmicks, and outdated scripts, it's easy to lose sight of what really moves people to say yes. That's why this book introduces you to a different approach, a deeper approach that will give you greater control in your sales presentations.

This is the *MindSell Model*: a simple, powerful, influence-based framework for transforming your sales performance. It's not a series of pressure tactics, nor a script from the 1990s dusted off and rebranded. It's not about tricking customers into buying things they don't want. Instead, it's a set of practical tools and strategies rooted in the timeless science of human behaviour, designed to help you sell smarter, connect deeper, and perform stronger, for both the short game and the long game.

> *When you understand the human mind,*
> *you stop fighting for sales and start leading*
> *customers to decisions they feel good about.*

You don't push them into buying. You create an environment where buying becomes the natural, empowered next step.

The MindSell Model is built around *seven essential pillars*. Each pillar strengthens a different dimension of your sales ability, guiding you to lead conversations that feel less like battles and more like natural collaborations.

Let's take a quick look at the seven pillars you're about to master:

1. Master Your Mindset: Starting Strong

Sales is a mental game first. You'll learn how to set your mind to win each day through the concepts of acceptance, total radical responsibility, and useful belief systems that fuel resilience.

2. The Power of Positioning: Why You?

Before you can influence others, you must anchor yourself. You'll craft a personal sales identity rooted in clarity, confidence, and resonance, making customers want to align with you.

3. Rapid Rapport: Tools for Instant Human Connection

Connection is currency. You'll harness body language, tone matching, and the power of curiosity to build instant emotional safety and make your clients feel comfortable.

4. Tailored Influence: Adapting Your Message to Match the Mind

There's no one-size-fits-all when it comes to influence.

You'll learn to adapt using colour personalities and behavioural cues that help you meet people exactly where they are.

5. Strategic Curiosity: The Art of Asking Great Questions

Asking the right questions at the right time is an art form. You'll discover elegant questioning frameworks that uncover true needs, hidden fears, and buying drivers.

6. Win the Short Game and the Long Game: Closing the Sale and Building the Relationship

Some deals close today. Some seeds take years to bear fruit. You'll master striking the balance between daily discipline and building a lifetime of trusted client relationships.

7. Sunset Goal Setting: Designing a Life of Excellence

This isn't just about hitting monthly quotas. You'll learn how to set goals that drive meaning, focus, and fulfillment in your personal and professional life.

Each pillar blends cutting-edge principles from behavioural psychology, neuroscience, and real-world influence strategies. Every idea is practical, actionable, and designed to be used in the heat of the moment when it matters most.

WHY THIS MATTERS MORE NOW THAN EVER

Sales is evolving at lightning speed. Today's buyers are bombarded with options, overwhelmed by information, and suspicious of anything that feels slick or self-serving. Attention spans are shorter. Competition is fierce. Trust is harder to earn and easier to lose.

But what hasn't changed is the core human need underneath it all. People still want to feel heard, seen, valued, and respected. They want someone who understands the world through their eyes and can help guide them safely through the complexity of decision-making.

The salesperson who wins today isn't just the one with the best product. It's the one who connects with emotional intelligence, leads with genuine insight, and builds trust quickly and authentically.

Welcome to *MindSell*.

You don't need a psychology degree to change the way you sell. You just need to understand how human beings work and honour them in the process. In the pages ahead, you'll find the tools, strategies, and mindset shifts that turn average sellers into trusted advisors, lifelong partners, and leaders of influence.

PART
ONE

MASTER YOUR MINDSET

◎ STARTING STRONG

Before we dive into scripts, strategies, or sales tools, we must start with something even more important: your headspace.

Some days, you feel like you're on top of the world, closing deals, feeling unstoppable and energised by every conversation. Other days, you're dragging yourself forward, wondering if you've lost your edge. That's not a flaw. That's not a sign you're in the wrong career. It's completely normal. If there's one universal constant in this game, it's uncertainty.

Some people spend their entire careers resisting it, wishing for things to feel safer, more predictable, and controlled. But the truth is, uncertainty isn't going anywhere. It's built into the DNA of selling. Which means if you want to thrive, you can't fight it. You must make peace with it.

And it all starts with the first critical move: *acceptance.*

Before anything can change in your sales results, something must change internally. It's critical to stop blaming external factors for any lack of success. Many salespeople are guilty of not taking responsibility for their results. Instead, they blame others. Let's face it – it's easier to blame the market, your boss, territory, company, competitors, the economy, latest tech disruption, algorithm, traffic, weather, or phase of the moon.

Blame is a mental prison, and taking ownership is the key to the door.

The moment you stop blaming others for your results, your sales career ignites, and we can begin to take this journey together. Taking ownership for your results isn't a burden; it's freedom from all the things that are holding you back. When you take ownership of your situation, you reclaim your power. You stop waiting for better conditions, and you start creating better outcomes. You stop making excuses, and you start making moves. You shift from being a passenger to being the driver.

Once you stop blaming other factors, you step into a new space: *adventure mindset.*

Adventure mindset transforms panic into presence, fear into forward motion, and obstacles into opportunities. When you treat your career like an adventure, uncertain and unfolding in real time, you unlock your deepest reserves of resilience and resourcefulness.

I think about white-water rafting trips I've taken in New Zealand. It's breathtakingly beautiful. At the start, the waters are usually very calm, relaxing and scenic. But when the raft hits the rapids, everything inside you wakes up. Your senses sharpen, and your instincts take over. Your heart pounds in your chest, and you become *fully alive.* The calm stretches of the river are nice, but it's the white water you really remember. It's the rapids that shape you.

Sales works in a very similar way. Overcoming the challenges and uncertainties, and doing the hard work is what you remember. It's what shapes you as a salesperson.

It's important to reframe the anxiety that comes with being a salesperson. While it's easier to focus on the anxiety and engage in catastrophic thinking about our challenges, we can also make a conscious decision to turn that anxiety into excitement. The white water of selling can either drive you into a state of fear, or we can reframe it as a challenge to succeed. Remember, the achievements you're most proud of in your life weren't easy – they were hard. That's why you're proud of them. You persevered, overcame the challenge, and won.

Incredibly, your body doesn't know the difference

between anxiety and excitement. Studies show that the physiological signals are nearly identical.[2] Your heart rate speeds up; your focus sharpens, and your adrenaline kicks in. The only real difference is the story you're telling yourself about what's happening. The most important words you say all day are the words you say to yourself, about yourself, when you're by yourself. In those moments, most people are cruel to themselves. That's what we must be aware of and change.

I've been speaking, coaching, and training sales teams for 25 years and have done 2,700 presentations around the world. In all that time, I've noticed something. Ultimately, there's one thing that separates the best salespeople from everybody else. The best salespeople in the world see opportunity in every market. They walk into every situation and figure out how they're going to succeed and make money. Average people see tough times. When you see tough times, your brain shuts down.

The research backs this up. Using simple reframing has a massive effect on performance. A 2013 study out of Harvard Business School, led by Alison Wood Brooks, found that individuals who consciously reinterpreted their anxiety as excitement performed significantly better under pressure. They performed better in public speaking, singing, and math tests.[3] Same body. Different story. Different outcome.

So, next time you feel that rush of anxiety, the butterflies and the racing heart before a big call or meeting, don't shrink from it. Take a deep breath and be conscious of what's happening. This is the time to control the words you say to yourself and see the opportunity, not the pressure. "This is exciting. This is my body getting ready to perform."

Then comes the joy and excitement of paddling through the rapids.

TOTAL RADICAL RESPONSIBILITY AND USEFUL BELIEF

There comes a moment in every successful career, and every successful life, when the real transformation begins. It's not the day you land the biggest client or win the biggest trophy. It's not the promotion, the big yearly bonus, or the headline moment that everyone notices. It's quieter than that. It's the moment you stop looking outward for answers and start looking inward for power.

That moment is called *total radical responsibility*.

Not partial responsibility. Not conditional ownership that only shows up when things are easy. But rather *total radical ownership*. Today, most people spend their lives pointing outward. They blame the economy, the company, the leadership team, the competition, even the customer who didn't call back. They create endless stories to explain why they aren't where they want to be. In doing so, they unknowingly surrender their power to forces they can't control.

But when you decide that everything in your life – from your habits, reactions, and results – is yours to own, something extraordinary happens. You stop waiting for things to get better. You start making them better. You stop hoping for the world to change. You start becoming the force that changes your world. Total radical responsibility isn't a burden. It's not a shackle. It's the ultimate freedom. It places you squarely back at the centre of your own life, not at the mercy of circumstances, but as the architect of your future.

Psychology supports this shift profoundly. American psychologist Julian Rotter's famous research on locus of control explored an individual's belief about the degree to which they have control over the events in their lives. He identified two main types: internal and external locus of control. Individuals with an internal locus of control believe their actions directly influence outcomes, while those with an external locus of control believe outcomes are largely determined by external factors such as luck or fate. The research showed that individuals who believe outcomes are shaped by their own actions consistently outperform those who feel life simply happens to them.[4]

Total radical responsibility doesn't mean ignoring challenges. It means refusing to be defined by them. It means standing in front of your life, no matter what storm is raging around you, and saying, "This is mine to shape." It's the shift from powerless to powerful, and it changes everything.

Ownership is freedom. In your sales career, you are the master of your own destiny, and by taking *total radical responsibility*, you build a solid foundation. Once you've done that, having a *useful belief* mindset is the rocket fuel that lifts everything off the ground.

Useful belief isn't just another motivational tool. It's not a feel-good phrase to stick on your wall or a bumper sticker slogan for hard days. It's a philosophy. It's a practical way of seeing the world that has transformed not just results, but entire lives.

I wrote the book *Useful Belief: Because It's Better than*

Positive Thinking back in 2016. It has been the subject of hundreds of my keynote speeches and coaching conversations, and I'm proud to say my bestselling book has impacted people across industries and the globe.

Useful Belief was born from a simple but profound realization: positive thinking doesn't work.

Positive thinking demands that you 'feel good'. It requires a certain emotional state. The fact is feelings are notoriously unreliable. When life is good, positive thinking is easy. But when life throws you into the rapids, when sales dry up, when the economy tightens, when rejection stings, positivity often collapses under the weight of reality.

Useful belief, on the other hand, doesn't require you to feel good. It only asks that you choose the belief that's most useful for moving forward. Positive thinking is emotional thinking. Obviously, negative thinking is also emotional thinking. Useful thinking is practical. It's pragmatic and delivers results. Useful belief doesn't argue with reality. It doesn't insist that everything is perfect. It simply asks, "Given the situation, what belief would be most useful to hold right now?"

Useful belief invites you to see life differently. Not with rose-coloured glasses, but with a lens sharpened by pragmatism and hope. It teaches you to program your mind with instructions that serve your goals, not your fears. If you believe now is the best time in history to be selling, you show up differently. You move with energy. You create opportunities others can't even see. If you believe your customers are impossible to deal with and your prospecting leads are dead, your mind will find proof of that too. Every day, you're teaching your mind what to look for. Useful belief simply makes sure you're teaching it something worth finding.

The psychology behind useful belief is powerful. It ties directly into the work pioneered by Aaron T. Beck, widely regarded as the father of cognitive therapy. Beck's work, particularly in the 1960s, focused on how negative thought patterns contribute to mental health issues like depression. He helped patients identify and challenge these negative thoughts, leading to improved emotional well-being.[5] Beck's methods laid the groundwork for 'cognitive reframing', a term used to describe the broader process of changing how someone perceives and interprets events, situations, or experiences. This involves reinterpreting negative thoughts and perspectives in a more positive or constructive way. Reframing teaches us that our interpretation of events, not the events themselves, shapes our emotional and behavioural responses.

Useful belief sharpens this idea into a practical tool you can use daily. It's not fake positivity. It's practical optimism, which leads to greater resilience. Useful belief is seeing the world through a lens that empowers action, even when circumstances challenge you.

Examples of useful beliefs include:

- This is the best time in the history of the world to be in my industry.

- This is the best time in the history of the world to be in sales.

- I love being a salesperson!

- Opportunities are everywhere in this market.

- Life begins at (insert age).

- This is the best time in the history of the world to be alive.

- I'm open to the technological advances within my industry.

- Every day is a gift, and I'll start every day with gratitude.

There are obviously so many more. The premise is you're completely in charge of filtering what you 'say' and what you 'see' in the world. Many people believe in 'tough times'. They love to tell you how tough things are, and their brain filter works to strengthen that belief. If you believe in tough times, you'll see the negative everywhere. You'll come up with excuses for lack of performance and start believing things were better in the past. We hear people talk about it all the time – how life was 'better' back then.

That type of thinking simply isn't useful. This is the best time in the history of the world to be alive. When you believe that, your brain sees the beauty in the world and your experiences, and opportunities appear.

It doesn't mean there aren't difficult parts of your job. There are. It also doesn't mean bad things don't happen. They do. Bad things happen to good people. That's reality. Sometimes in life it's important to make a change – not everything is designed to last forever. Sometimes quitting something that's not working in your life is a positive action. You can make that decision. However, and this is most important, if you're not going to change a perceived negative aspect of your life, or can't change it, you might as well reframe it and have a useful belief about it. If this is your reality, what's the most useful belief you can have about the situation?

BRINGING IT ALL TOGETHER

You've now built the kind of mindset foundation very few people ever even glimpse, let alone master. You've accepted that uncertainty isn't something to fight, but rather something to ride. You've embraced having an *adventure mindset*, seeing the unknown rapids not as anxiety, but rather as excitement. You've also claimed *total radical responsibility*, taking full ownership, giving you both freedom and power. To top it all off, you've installed *useful belief*, programming your mind for momentum rather than paralysis.

> *Mastering your mindset isn't just about selling more; it's about living your life better. It's about becoming the kind of person people want to follow, not because you shout louder, but because you walk stronger.*

Sales is a mental game before it's ever a conversation. Winners master acceptance, adventure mindset, total radical responsibility, and useful belief to stay resilient, focused, and strong every day. Each interaction begins with the mindset you bring to it.

PART
TWO

THE POWER OF POSITIONING

◎ WHY YOU?

Let's begin with a question every salesperson must be able to answer instantly, confidently, and without hesitation: *Why you?*

Why should someone choose you over anyone else? You must be able to answer that question. Not in a rehearsed, robotic, product-flogging way, but in a way that resonates from deep inside because the best salespeople don't convince themselves they're adding value. They already know they are. They know, without a shadow of a doubt, what separates them from the pack.

A true value-adding salesperson is aligned with a greater sense of purpose. They're proud of their profession. They show up with conviction, not just to hit targets but to create impact. They aren't just selling products; they're offering transformations, solutions, and real partnerships. They understand their services inside and out, but even more importantly, they know the energy, commitment, and excellence they personally bring to the table. It's not arrogance, but rather it's congruence. And it's magnetic.

Ask yourself, have you ever actually stopped to write down your answer to 'why you?' Not just thought about it casually, but seriously crafted it. Have you ever shaped it into something you can live and breathe in every client interaction? If not, now's the time. Think about what your clients consistently praise you for. Reflect on what you do better than 90 percent of people in your industry. Imagine your longest-standing client having to persuade someone else to work with you. What would they say?

This process is important because when you can articulate your unique value cleanly, honestly, and powerfully, you transform how you sell. You no longer fumble through features or drown in discount wars. You lead with certainty. And certainty sells.

Imagine walking into a client meeting where they look you in the eye and ask, "Why should we go with you?" Your answer isn't a nervous list of services or a string of rehearsed buzzwords. Instead, it's a simple confident story. You separate yourself not by shouting louder, but by standing clearer.

A great exercise, which I recommend every salesperson

does, is to ask five of your best clients why they love working with you. Listen carefully to their answers. Look for patterns. You might find that your real edge isn't what you thought it was. It might not be your technical expertise. It might be your ability to simplify complexity, your speed of communication, your consistency, or simply the way you make people feel safe and heard. More often than not, the real reason people stay with you isn't the product. It's how you make them feel during the process.

At a deeper level, knowing 'why you?' makes you personally stronger and taps directly into the core of what drives human motivation. It connects to a powerful framework in psychology known as self-determination theory (SDT), developed in the 1980s by psychologists Edward Deci and Richard Ryan. According to SDT, people perform at their best and are motivated, resilient, and fulfilled when three basic psychological needs are met: autonomy, competence, and relatedness.[6]

When you get clear on your positioning in sales, you fire up all three. First, you claim *autonomy* by defining your own narrative. In other words, you're not just repeating what your company brochure says, but rather you're crafting your voice, your difference, and your promise. You step into *competence* because reflecting on your strengths reminds you that you're capable, competent, and have earned the right to be successful. Finally, you foster *relatedness* because you're not simply offering a transaction, but rather you're offering a relationship built on understanding, reliability, and care.

This work matters because buyers today aren't just looking for solutions. They're looking for certainty. They're looking for someone who can guide them, reduce complexity, and help them make a good decision and feel good about it.

In a world overflowing with options, people aren't just choosing based on features and benefits anymore. They're choosing based on who they feel understands them and who they feel they can trust.

In this environment, sameness is invisible. If you cannot clearly articulate your 'why you?' you risk blending into the noise. And in a noisy world, the easiest comparison customers make is price. When they can't distinguish quality, they default to cost.

But when you've done the work to own your value, shape your message, and deliver it authentically, you don't have to fight for attention. You command it. And it's not because you're louder. It's because you're clearer. People are drawn to clarity the way ships are drawn to a lighthouse. They trust it. They move toward it.

Positioning isn't about puffing yourself up. It's not about spin. It's about getting brutally honest about what you offer that's real, rare, and valuable, and then bringing that truth to life with humility and pride.

Owning your 'why you?' isn't a script to memorise. It's a truth to embody. The best salespeople in the world possess two things: certainty and simplicity. They're certain about their message, and they deliver that message in a simple way. No one buys when they're confused.

EQUALISE THEN SEPARATE

In today's noisy hypercompetitive world, separation isn't enough. Everyone is shouting. Everyone is claiming to be faster, better, smarter. Features are stacked on features. Claims are piled on top of claims. In that chaos, it's easy for customers to get overwhelmed. And when people are overwhelmed, they don't act. They stall. They delay. They default to deciding based on the simplest factor they know, which is price.

That's the reality every modern salesperson is walking into. And it's why mastering the principle of *equalise then separate* is no longer just important; it's essential.

Equalise then separate is one of the most practical,

elegant, and transformational communication strategies in the entire sales world. When used well, it changes the emotional temperature of the conversation. It lowers the client's defences. It builds trust in seconds. Most importantly, it frames your true points of difference in a way that feels genuine, respectful, and impossible to ignore.

Thousands of salespeople who have learned this technique have transformed their results and their careers. It's one of the most important moves in the MindSell playbook.

WHAT MOST SALESPEOPLE DO WRONG

Most salespeople, under pressure to win business, start by trying to separate themselves from the competition. They rush into differentiation before they've earned the right to lead. It sounds something like this:

- "Our system is faster."

- "Our pricing is better."

- "Our customer service is world-class."

- "We're the only ones who do X, Y, Z."

The problem? From the customer's perspective, it all sounds the same. Everyone says they're the best. Everyone claims to be different. And when everyone claims to be different, ironically, no one is. The customer doesn't feel impressed. They feel suspicious.

In fact, early self-promotion without trust building can trigger the feeling of being sold to or manipulated. When that happens, buyers lean back emotionally. They become sceptical, cautious, and resistant. And when buyers feel resistance? They start comparing, usually focusing on the easiest thing to compare: price. This creates the deadly trap where you get caught defending your value instead of confidently offering it.

That's why equalise then separate is such a powerful antidote. It doesn't just work better; it works because it follows how the human brain makes decisions. It's all about sequence. Let's look at how it works.

Firstly, you *equalise* with the opposition. You begin by calmly acknowledging what you and your competitors share. You affirm the obvious in that there are many good providers in the market and customers have real choices. The other companies can, in fact, do some things as well as you do. You're evening up the playing field. At this point, you're happy if the customer sees you as the same as the competition. This simple move disarms the customer. It also shows the salesperson's maturity and security. Most importantly, it builds immediate trust.

Secondly, once you've created that trust, it's now time for you to *separate* from the competitor. This is so important. You highlight one or two meaningful ways that you or your offer is different. But you don't do it randomly; you separate specifically around what the client values most. You don't blast 15 points of difference at them. Instead, you choose the differences that matter to them, their goals, and their challenges.

In a real estate example, the first two parts of equalise and separate may sound a bit like this:

"The reality is there are some excellent agents working in this area. There are many agents who could be competent in selling your home. After all, we all have access to the **same** advertising tools, photographers, and online platforms. It's very much the **same**. The agents all have some good salespeople, nice offices, and informative websites. The thing, however, that's very **different**, what my clients consistently tell me matters, and what truly **separates** me from competitors is communication. It's the thing you said was most important for you in the selection of an agent. Let me share with you how I communicate and how you have access to any information you want twenty-four hours a day so you're never left wondering what's happening."

This opens a corridor for you to discuss the process in which you use technology for real-time reporting, face-to-face meetings, and frequent call updates to make sure the seller never feels like they're left in the dark.

Finally, you connect that difference directly to the *benefit* the client ultimately cares about. This is your opportunity in the real estate example to link how better communication will lead to a better result and more money for the seller. Ultimately, to have maximum impact in winning the business, the process must lead to what the seller really wants.

The same strategy works beautifully in B2B sales. I once coached a team selling software solutions to mid-sized companies. Their competitors had similar platforms, similar features, similar pricing, and similar integration times. Their reps used to walk into meetings with their guns blazing:

- "Here's why our product is better!"

- "Here's why our dashboard is better!"

- "Here's why our AI is smarter!"

The competition was saying the same things. It wasn't working, so we needed to change the approach. We needed to go in with equalise then separate.

"There are some outstanding platforms in this space. Frankly, on paper, we probably all look **similar**. Where we tend to hear we're **different**, and where our clients tell us it matters most, is how we stay involved after implementation. Our team doesn't disappear once the contract is signed. We're still there six months later, on weekly calls, and the **benefit** to you is we're helping your team optimise the project. The **result** is that our support saves our clients a great deal of time, money, and frustration."

Once again, this process has led to what the customer really wants. In this case, it's ongoing support that ultimately leads to a greater overall result. Nothing else had changed. Not the product. Not the price. Just the story. In summary, here's the process:

Step 1: Equalise

Calmly acknowledge common ground with competitors. This shows confidence, maturity, and lowers the defences of the customer.

Step 2: Separate

After equalizing, highlight how you and your company

are different from the competition, based on what matters most to the client.

Step 3: Benefit

Show how that separation will ultimately lead to a better result for the customer.

Another simple example:

"A lot of providers in our industry offer excellent service. Most have **similar** technology. Where we tend to **stand apart** is in our post-sale support, ongoing optimization, and hands-on partnership. For you, that means the **benefit** is faster adoption, smoother rollouts, and better ROI in the first year."

COMMON MISTAKES MADE BY SALESPEOPLE

Here's where most salespeople make mistakes with equalise then separate:

- They separate too early.

- They try to separate features that should really be equalised because they're the same.

- They separate on things the customer doesn't really care about.

If you rush to separate without building trust first, you look desperate. If you blast the customer with too many differences, you create confusion. If you highlight a feature they don't value, you lose relevance. Keep it simple. Once again, nobody buys when they're confused.

PART THREE

RAPID RAPPORT

◎ TOOLS FOR INSTANT HUMAN CONNECTION

In today's fast-paced world of selling, there's no luxury of time to slowly earn trust over months of gentle interactions. You have minutes and sometimes seconds. Building instant rapport isn't just helpful anymore; it's a necessity. And the truth is, *matching skills* provide the fastest path to gaining rapid rapport.

What are matching skills? Matching is one of the most powerful tools in human communication, but like anything powerful, it must be understood and used right. It's not about mimicking or pretending. It's about stepping into someone's world, genuinely and respectfully, and speaking their language. Not just with words, but with tone, posture, energy, and rhythm. Matching is about creating an unconscious emotional safety signal that says, "You're seen. You're safe. You can trust me." When that happens, influence follows naturally.

Human beings are biologically programmed to trust those who seem familiar. Our brains are constantly scanning for signals of 'like me' or 'not like me'. This isn't conscious, but rather it's primal. When someone subtly mirrors our energy, tone, and pace, we instinctively lean toward them. We relax. We listen. This is known in psychology as the 'law of familiarity'. Matching taps into this deep, hardwired need for connection. It creates what psychologists call neurolinguistic alignment, which is a synchronization of communication at an unconscious level where conversation flows more freely and influence feels effortless.

Supporting this, one of the most cited studies in the history of communication comes from Professor Albert Mehrabian of UCLA. His groundbreaking research found that when it comes to communicating feelings and attitudes, only 7 percent of meaning comes from the actual words spoken; 38 percent comes from tone of voice, and a staggering 55 percent comes from body language.[7] In other words, *93 percent of your impact happens before your words are even fully processed*. It's not what you say, but rather how you say it. It's your tone, pace, posture, and presence.

This is why matching is so essential. It allows you to tap into that 93 percent with intention. It allows you to move beyond mere logic and enter the emotional space where real trust is built. Matching isn't manipulation. Done properly, it's mindful communication. It's the art of stepping out of your own frame of reference and stepping into the emotional landscape of another person. This isn't to 'get' them, but to meet them with genuine presence and respect. It's one of the purest forms of empathy.

The science behind matching is deeper than comfort alone. Neuroscience tells us that mirror neurons play a crucial role in human connection. Mirror neurons are specialised cells that fire both when we perform an action, and when we observe someone else performing that same action. They're responsible for the contagiousness of yawns, the spread of laughter in a room, and the instinct to lean forward when someone else does. When you match another person's tone, posture, or rhythm naturally, their mirror neurons activate. Their brain unconsciously categorises you as 'safe', 'like me', and 'trustworthy'.

HOW DO WE MATCH OTHERS?

Building the skill of matching in daily life doesn't require magic, but rather simple awareness. Start today. When you meet someone new, pay attention to their energy level, their speaking speed, the way they sit or move. Don't imitate. Simply adjust lightly. Speak a little faster with fast talkers. Slow down slightly with slower speakers. Smile more if they smile easily. Small shifts create massive relational dividends.

Some of the best matchers I've ever seen don't even consider themselves salespeople. They're waiters, baristas, and everyday service staff who somehow 'get you' within moments. They pick up on your vibe without you having to say a word. They mirror your mood. They meet you emotionally. That's the power of matching. And it's why when you master it, you're no longer just selling; you're connecting at a human level that transcends transactions.

Every day that you walk into a meeting with a customer, you have a choice. You can communicate from your frame, or you can adapt and communicate into theirs. You can demand they come to your energy, or you can step into theirs with grace and mastery. One path creates resistance. The other opens doors.

The salespeople who master matching are the ones who create emotional ease quickly. They're the ones who customers trust faster, open to more willingly, and stay loyal to long after the contract is signed. They understand that influence isn't about pushing harder. It's about listening deeper. It's about caring enough to adjust, not just who you are but how you show up.

The more you practice matching, the more it becomes second nature. You'll find yourself noticing rhythms in conversations you once overlooked. You'll feel when someone needs you to slow down, or speed up, or bring a different energy into the room. And every time you make that adjustment mindfully and respectfully, you deepen the relationship.

A great way to see matching in action is to go to the pub. Watch men at the pub. What do they do? They order a beer, and a group often stands in a circle; they put their hands in their pockets, and they start rocking. Rocking back and forth, beer in hand. Rocking and talking. Talking and rocking. All matching because they relate to each other. What I want you to notice is that often there's one guy in the group who isn't matching the body language. They have flat feet; their knees are locked, and they have two hands on their beer glass. They look a little uncomfortable. They're in the group, but they're not really in the group. When we're connected, we're all doing the same thing.

Women are no different. You'll see a group of women all sitting and drinking champagne, legs crossed, chatting. Sitting and chatting. Once again, there's often one woman who isn't doing what everyone else is doing. She isn't matching body language. Her legs are off to one side, glass of champagne resting in her lap, and she looks slightly uncomfortable. Once again, while she is in the group, she isn't really in the group at this moment. When we're connected, even at an unconscious level, we're doing what everyone else is doing.

People in new love are the same. Watch a couple who are in love having an intense conversation and loving the process of getting to know each other. They're sitting across from each other. When one moves forward, the other moves forward. When one moves back, the other moves back. Back and forth. Together and apart. In sync and matching at an unconscious level.

You can also watch a couple who have been together longer than two years. One moves forward, but the other doesn't move!

While matching happens at an unconscious level when we have deep levels of rapport, we can also bring it into our conscious awareness and make the decision to match the customer. If they move forward, you move forward. If they lean back, when it's appropriate you can lean back. It doesn't have to be perfect. It's just adapting and adjusting body language with elegance and subtlety.

We do this naturally with children. If a five-year-old child walks into the room, you get down on their level with your body language and speak in a slower, higher tone to that child. You do this naturally. Why? You want that child to feel safe and comfortable in your presence.

It's no different with adults. Adapt and adjust body language and tone to make your customers feel safe and comfortable in your presence.

THE FORD FRAMEWORK

In a world where attention spans are shrinking and authentic connection is harder to come by, one framework rises quietly but powerfully above the noise: FORD.

Simple, elegant, and life-changing, FORD has helped thousands of salespeople move beyond transactions into true relationships, and it's just as powerful outside the boardroom as it is inside.

At its core, FORD isn't a sales tactic. It's a human connection blueprint. It's a philosophy about genuine curiosity. It's about caring enough to discover what matters most to the person across from you. Whether you're meeting a new client, leading a team, hosting a dinner party, or sitting next to a stranger on a plane, FORD just works. It's the art of selling, leadership, parenting, dating, small talk, database management, or simply conversation. It's a great all-round tool of communication. FORD stands for:

Family
Occupation
Relaxation
Dreams

These four areas tap into the emotional heartbeat of people's lives and their relationships, identity, passions, and future hopes. When you step into these conversations with presence and curiosity, you move from surface-level talk to meaningful connection. You don't just make a good impression. You make a lasting impact.

Why Ford Works

When you ask about family, occupation, relaxation, and dreams, you're tapping directly into what psychologists call intrinsic motivators. These are the activities and values people pursue for their own satisfaction, not because they must, but because they want to. When people share personal information, they naturally deepen their feelings of trust and affinity toward the listener. In other words, when you ask someone about their life, and truly listen, you create an emotional bridge faster than any pitch deck ever could.

Most importantly, 'active constructive responding',

a concept pioneered by psychologist Dr. Shelly Gable, teaches us that when someone shares something personal and you respond with genuine enthusiasm, curiosity, and support, the relationship strengthens dramatically.[8] FORD is built for this. It gives you a map for creating those moments when someone feels seen, valued, and uplifted.

In sales, where relationships often determine who wins the business, these psychological dynamics aren't just interesting, they're essential. Let's go through some examples of the FORD questions you may ask.

F = Family

Human beings are tribal creatures. Our relationships with family and close friends form the bedrock of our identity. That's why asking about family is such a powerful conversation starter. It creates a sense of familiarity, warmth, and humanity. You don't need to pry or get too personal. A simple sincere question works wonders:

- "So, are you from here originally?"

- "What brought you to this area?"

- "That's fantastic, how long have you been together?"

- "Wow. So how old are the kids now?"

- "What school do they go to?"

- "What suburb are you living in? How long have you been there?"

You get the idea. Obviously, the conversation will be adapted to where they take you with their answers. It's also possible they'll ask you 'F' questions as well. If they do, please answer them! Don't look at them and say, "I'm sorry, I can't answer that right now. I'm performing the FORD technique on you."

Family opens the heart. It's where the real conversations begin.

O = Occupation

Occupation is another natural comfortable doorway into connection. For many people, their work is a major part of their identity. Asking about it with genuine curiosity shows respect for what they dedicate so much of their life to. It will also give you tremendous insight into the type of person they are, and their personality type. Try questions like:

- "So, what is it you do for work?"

- "Fantastic. How did you get started in that?"

- "Obviously, there have been a lot of changes in that industry. How are you finding it?"

- "What's the plan moving forward? Do you think you will stay in it?"

- "That's great. It sounds like you are **busy**."

- I always finish the 'O' questions with the last one. Three words that are the best to gain rapport in the English language. *You are busy.* In Australia, acknowledging that someone is busy signals importance, achievement, relevance. It's a small phrase that carries big relational weight.

R = Relaxation

This is where the energy of the conversation often lifts as you ask about what they like to do in their free time. What do they like to do to relax? What are their hobbies, passions, and weekend plans? This is where you invite the customer to light up about what brings them joy. A few thoughtful questions may include:

- "So, when you're not doing all this, what do you like to do to get away from it all?"

- "I noticed the signed football jumper. Do you follow that team?"

- "You're obviously working hard. Any good breaks coming up? Any holiday plans?"

- "You mentioned you have a holiday house. Where is that? Do you get there a bit?"

- "I see the photo of you finishing that race. Is that a triathlon? When do you train?"

- Relaxation conversations move people from professional mode to personal mode. Once again, you can learn a lot about a customer by what fires them up in their free time. You may also find that you have many things in common, which can lead to bonding conversations and ideas for future touch points.

D = Dreams

Dreams are sacred territory. They represent someone's hopes, future, and inner aspirations. When a customer is willing to share something they're trying to achieve, and there's a sense of vulnerability, you know you've won them over. People only share dreams and vulnerability with people they trust. If you feel like the customer is sharing that vulnerability with you, asking dreams questions can be a great way to cement the relationship. Dream questions to consider are:

- "Where are you hoping to take this business into the future?"

- "What's the five-year plan of the company?"

- "What are you personally hoping to achieve with this result? What are the next steps?

- "How do you see us helping you achieve that outcome?"

- "What's your long-term investment plan? What would be your dream result?"

Dreams are where vulnerability shows up. People may reveal career ambitions, travel goals, creative projects, or legacy visions. When someone shares a dream, *you're being invited into their future*, which is an incredible honour. When you connect to someone's dream, you connect to their core identity. Deals are closed here. Partnerships are born here. Lifelong trust is created here.

WHY FORD IS MORE THAN JUST SMALL TALK

Small talk gets a bad reputation in the sales world. It's often dismissed as filler, fluff, or wasted time. But small talk, done strategically and sincerely through frameworks like FORD, is smart talk. It's the emotional scaffolding that real business is built on.

Research shows that people don't remember what you said nearly as much as how you made them feel.[9] Using FORD makes people feel heard, understood, and appreciated. That emotional resonance sticks longer than any clever pitch could.

Moreover, conversations rooted in FORD create *emotional memory anchors*. When someone associates you with a meaningful conversation about their child, their passion, or their dream, they remember you fondly and favourably. You're no longer just another salesperson. You're part of their emotional story.

PART
FOUR

TAILORED INFLUENCE

◎ ADAPTING YOUR MESSAGE TO MATCH THE MIND

In the art of influence, one size never fits all. If there's one fundamental truth in human communication, it's that people aren't the same. They don't think the same way. They don't decide the same way. They don't buy the same way. If you want to truly connect, persuade, and lead, you must do more than deliver your message clearly. You must adapt it, shaping how you communicate so it lands squarely in the world of the person sitting in front of you.

This ability to meet people in the way they need to be met is what separates good communicators from great ones. It's the difference between presenting ideas and moving people.

Over the years, there have been many attempts to categorise and understand personality. Systems like the DISC Profile have long been popular in the business world, classifying people into dominance, influence, steadiness, and conscientiousness types. Each letter or category represents a behavioural tendency that can guide how someone interacts, works, and makes decisions. Similarly, the Myers-Briggs Type Indicator (MBTI) has influenced generations of professionals, introducing the world to combinations like ENFP and ISTJ, and is rooted in Carl Jung's theories of psychological types.

These systems are valuable. They offer insight into human nature. But in the moment when you're sitting in front of a customer, leading a meeting, or navigating a crucial conversation, they can sometimes feel overly complex. You're unlikely to pull out a DISC chart in a heated negotiation or mentally run through sixteen Myers-Briggs types during a first sales call.

That's where this model, the Colour Personality Framework, proves uniquely powerful. It's simple. It's intuitive. It's incredibly practical. And most importantly, it works in real conversations.

Instead of sorting through endless acronyms, animal types, or rigid categories, you simply tune into four key personality colours: *red, yellow, aqua*, and *blue*. Each colour represents a distinct pattern of thinking, feeling, and deciding. You don't need a test result or a psychological report. You just need a bit of observation, a little intuition, and a willingness to meet people where they naturally are.

We begin with the red personalities, the drivers of the world. These are the individuals who move fast, think about the future, and operate with a laser-focused intensity that can electrify a room, and can also bulldoze it. Understanding how to speak the language of a red can be the difference between being ignored entirely and truly inspiring decisive action.

From there, we'll explore the visionary yellows, the grounded aquas, and the meticulous blues, with each one having their own beautiful, sometimes challenging, but always fascinating approach to life and business.

Learning to read these colours and adapt accordingly isn't about labelling people or putting them into boxes. It's about opening new doors of connection. It's about honouring the fact that everyone experiences the world differently and true influence begins when you meet them on their terms, not yours.

So, as we step into this section of the book, remember that this isn't just about selling better. It's also about seeing people better. It's about building bridges where others build barriers. And when you master that art, you don't just close deals; you open lifelong relationships.

RED PERSONALITY: THE POWERHOUSE MINDSET

Reds are the drivers of the world. These are your powerhouses, the ones who create momentum in any room they enter. They're bold, focused, and unapologetically driven. Reds aren't here to make friends as much as they're here to make progress. There's an intensity to them that can feel electric, or intimidating, depending on your personality type. But make no mistake, when you're face-to-face with a red you'll feel it in the air. They don't just attend meetings; they take command of the room.

Reds are obsessed with outcomes. They're not thinking about the process unless that process gets them closer to the result. These are the CEOs who cut meetings short, the entrepreneurs who launch before everything is perfect, the elite performers who aren't trying to be liked, but rather they're trying to win.

But while their forward motion can be impressive, it can also make them seem impatient, abrasive, or even intimidating. This isn't personal, but rather it's just how they're wired. Their focus is fixed on the finish line.

How to Spot a Red in the Wild

Red personalities don't always wear red jackets or shout from the rooftops. But they leave unmistakable clues in how they operate. Here are some key signs:

- **Short communication**: You get emails that say *Approved* or *4 p.m. fine*. No fluff, no emojis, no signoffs.

- **Decision speed**: Reds decide fast. They don't need every piece of information. They'll move with 70 percent of the data and fix things later if needed.

- **Low tolerance for rambling**: They'll fidget in meetings, check their phones, or cut people off if they sense they're not getting to the point.

- **Result-oriented questions**: They ask things like, "What's the ROI?", "How fast?" or, "What's the bottom line?"

You'll feel it. Whether you're pitching, presenting, or just trying to have a conversation – Reds move quickly, and they expect you to keep up.

How to Sell to a Red

Selling to a red isn't about warming them up; it's about matching their energy. If you try to lead with rapport building and stories, you'll lose them. Reds don't care about your weekend, your dog, or where you went on holiday. They care about what you're offering and whether it will move the needle.

Here's your red-friendly approach:

- **Get to the point immediately**: Lead with the outcome. "This strategy will increase your close rate by fifteen percent in thirty days." That's your opener.

- **Use bullet points**: Structure matters. They don't want paragraphs; they want headlines. If you can't explain it in five words or less, you're at risk.

- **Focus on ROI, speed, and results**: Talk in outcomes, timeframes, and competitive advantage.

- **Speak with confidence**: Uncertainty is a deal-breaker for reds. If you don't believe in what you're offering, they won't either.

The Challenge with Reds

Let's be honest – reds aren't always easy to work with. They can come across as blunt, cold, or even rude. But that's not what's happening. They're just driven by a different operating system.

Reds aren't trying to be mean; they're trying to make things happen.

When a red cuts you off in a meeting, it's not personal. When they respond with, *Not interested* to your carefully written email, it's not because they dislike you. It's because they're moving too fast to slow down.

This is where a useful belief mindset shift is crucial.

Useful Belief for Working with Reds

"They're not being rude, they're being results-driven. I'm here to match that energy and help them win."

This belief changes the game. It puts you in a place of strength instead of defensiveness. Rather than getting frustrated by their pace, you lean into it. You work *with* it. If you treat a red like a problem, they'll feel it, and they'll move on. But if you meet them with clarity, confidence, and speed, they'll trust you. And once a red trusts you, you're in their inner circle.

Questions to Ask Yourself

Let's turn the mirror around:

- Who are the reds in your life or business?

- Are they a challenge for you, or are you energised by them?

- Do you resist their pace, or are you willing to match their intensity?

- Working with reds isn't about changing them; it's about adapting *you*. And when you can do that, you unlock one of the most powerful forms of influence: meeting someone where they are and leading from there.

YELLOW PERSONALITY: THE EMOTIONAL ENGINE

If reds are the bullet trains of the business world with straight lines, speed, and being destination-focused, then yellows are the hot-air balloons. They're colourful, uplifting, unpredictable, and full of stories. Yellows are experience seekers. They're connectors, creators, and collaborators. They thrive on energy, joy, and most of all, people.

When a yellow walks into the room, you'll know it. They're the ones lighting up every corner with laughter, stories, hugs, and want everyone around them to feel good. Yellows aren't chasing a result like reds, but rather they're chasing a feeling. They're the personalities who ask, *How does this feel?* and, *Do I want to do this?* They don't necessarily think about, *What does this cost?* or, *What's the return on investment?* They don't just want to win; they also want to enjoy the process of winning.

Yellows are fuelled by excitement. Not just in

achieving a goal, but in the anticipation of something fun. Yellows are constantly scanning the horizon for what's new, interesting, and inspiring. They're emotion-first decision-makers and are more prone to impulse decisions. That's your yellow.

How to Spot a Yellow in the Wild

So how do you recognise a yellow? Here are the dead giveaways:

- **They're expressive**: You'll see emojis, exclamation marks, and creative flourishes in every message.

- **They talk a lot**: They love to tell stories, veer off topic, and often have several ideas bubbling at once, and you're going to get the long version of the story.

- **They're magnetic**: They smile, hug, light up the virtual call, and make everyone feel part of something.

- **They get distracted**: You'll be mid-conversation, and suddenly they're asking about something seemingly unrelated.

How to Sell to a Yellow

Selling to a yellow is less of a pitch and more of an

experience. They don't want a spreadsheet; rather they want a conversation. They want to be inspired. If your product or service makes their life feel easier, more joyful, or more exciting, you're more likely to win the business.

Here's your yellow-friendly approach:

- **Be enthusiastic**: Match their energy. Come in alive. If you're flat, they'll tune out.

- **Use stories and metaphors**: Don't just say what it does, describe how it *feels* to use it.

- **Focus on experience**: "You're going to *love* how this works." "This will make your day so much easier." Paint the picture.

- **Compliment their ideas**: Say things like, "That's such a cool way to look at it." Yellows need to feel seen.

The Challenge with Yellows

Let's talk about the flip side. While they can be super enthusiastic, yellows can also display characteristics of people who have a lot going on in their brain.

The greatest challenge in dealing with yellows is they can be disorganised. They can forget calls, miss follow-ups, and can double-book themselves. They can be inconsistent and change their mind quickly. You might have a great call; then when you try to follow that up, you get nothing back.

Yellows can also be overly optimistic and may commit to more than they can handle. All of it means you must be diligent in your follow-up. Just because you received a verbal go-ahead, it doesn't mean they won't change their mind.

With yellows, it's important to have the right useful belief mindset.

Useful Belief for Working with Yellows

"They're not being flaky, they're fast-moving and feeling-driven. If I stay enthusiastic and can present value in a fun way, I'll keep them engaged."

Yellows are impulse buyers, but that doesn't mean they're careless. They simply trust their *gut*. If something feels right, they'll say yes on the spot. But don't forget emotional momentum can fade just as quickly as it started.

Yellows are your fastest close, and potentially your fastest churn. They're prone to buyer evaporation, which isn't remorse, but distraction. If they don't feel energised post purchase, they'll drift. That's why post-sale engagement with a yellow needs to keep the vibe alive.

Questions to Ask Yourself

Let's bring it home with a few reflection points:

- Who are the yellows in your life or business?

- Do you embrace their energy or get frustrated by it?

- What would it look like to build your sales presentation around excitement and emotion, not just information?

- Yellows are your bright sparks. They're the ones who bring life to the meeting, light to the message, and laughter to the follow-up. Selling to them isn't about perfect delivery. Instead, it's about creating a memorable emotional *experience*.

AQUA PERSONALITY: THE ANCHOR IN THE STORM

If red is the driver and yellow is the spark, aqua is the calm in the storm. When the room is spinning and the energy is peaking, aqua personalities are the ones grounding everyone with quiet strength and unwavering presence. They're not trying to win the spotlight. They're trying to create *harmony*. And in a world obsessed with fast, flashy, and loud, aquas are a breath of fresh air.

These are the nicest, kindest people in the world. They're your peacekeepers, the people who lead through empathy, observation, and consistency. Aquas don't need to raise their voice to be heard. They don't need to dominate a conversation to shape its direction. They operate in a different gear that's slower, more thoughtful, intentional, and nonconfrontational. But don't mistake their softness for weakness. Aquas are strong in a way that doesn't shout. They show up. They stay. They're loyal.

How to Spot an Aqua in the Wild

You won't find an aqua by looking for the loudest person in the room. You'll find them by watching the ones who stay steady. Their characteristics include:

- **They speak softly**: Calm tones, warm eyes, slower pacing.

- **They rarely interrupt**: Instead, they listen all the way through and reflect.

- **They think before speaking**: Silence doesn't mean discomfort or disagreement. It means they're processing the information you gave them.

- **They avoid confrontation**: If tension arises, they might withdraw or say nothing.

Aqua personalities are often the ones others go to when things fall apart. They're the 'safe harbor' friends. The teammates who remember birthdays and ask how your mum's surgery went. Their superpower? They care.

How to Sell to an Aqua

Selling to an aqua is about building *emotional safety*. If a red wants control and a yellow wants excitement, an aqua wants *reassurance*.

Here's your playbook:

- **Don't pressure**: Aquas will withdraw instantly if they feel pressured or rushed.

- **Ask open-ended reflective questions**: "How does that feel to you?" or, "What would make this easier for you?"

- **Give them time**: If they say, "I'll think about it," trust them. That *is* part of their decision process.

- **Focus on values**: Talk about service, support, longevity, reliability. They're buying the relationship.

- When presenting, keep your tone calm and grounded. Don't come in too hot. Speak with kindness and certainty. If you push, they'll pull away. But if you create space, they'll walk toward you.

The Challenge with Aquas

Aquas aren't always easy to read. They rarely say "no" outright. Instead, they'll say things like, "Let me think about it" or, "I'm not sure yet" or famously, "I just need a bit more time." This can be confusing, especially for high-speed salespeople who are used to quick decisions. This is where your mindset comes in.

Aquas are more naturally wired to seek calm, regulate stress, and avoid threats. What drives them isn't adrenaline, but rather it's trust. Their brains are more responsive to signals of emotional safety and relational consistency. They typically don't react quickly. That isn't because they're indecisive, but because they want to get it right. They're scanning for sincerity, steadiness, and respect.

Useful Belief for Working with Aquas

"They're not indecisive, they're careful and considerate. When they commit, it means something. My patience builds trust."

Aquas may also avoid hard conversations. If there's

something they don't like, they may not tell you directly. That's why it's important to check in gently and often. They make decisions based on internal values, not external metrics. These individuals seek authenticity, emotional safety, and inner alignment. They're deeply empathetic, often attuned to the emotional needs of others before even addressing their own.

Questions to Ask Yourself

Let's bring it home with some reflection:

- Who are the aquas in your life or business?

- Are you honouring their pace or trying to rush them?

- Do you create a sense of emotional safety in your follow-up, or do you add pressure?

- Aquas remind us that business is still human. Selling to them isn't about flashy presentations or clever closes. It's about showing up, being real, and building something that lasts.

BLUE PERSONALITY:
THE ARCHITECT OF EXCELLENCE

If red is the driver, yellow is the spark, and aqua is the calm, blue is the blueprint – the mind that maps the path, plots the course, checks for weak spots, and won't move forward until the foundations are solid. While other personalities rush in or float through, the blue personality stays grounded, strategic, structured, and serious about getting things *right*.

Blues are the planners, the perfectionists, the people who ask "how?" and "why?" before they say yes. They're detail-driven logic-first thinkers who don't get swept up in hype or emotion. They're moved by process, preparation, and proof.

At their core, blues want clarity, accuracy, and certainty. If something's going to be done, it should be done well, or not at all. These are individuals who process the world internally, guided by logic, structure, and a desire to systemise their understanding of things. Blues often seek control – not over others, but over the *process*.

Psychologically, they're risk averse. Blues want facts. They want to understand. They want to reduce uncertainty before acting. From a neuroscience perspective, they likely show heightened prefrontal cortex activity, which is responsible for rational thinking, planning, and decision-making. Emotional appeals, high-pressure tactics, and 'just trust me' vibes won't work here. Blues need the *what*, the *how*, and especially the *why* spelled out, step by step.

How to Spot a Blue in the Wild

Blues don't need to announce themselves. You'll feel it in the way they *organise* their questions and how they *process* your answers.

Here's how to recognise a blue:

- They ask a lot of clarifying questions to make sure they understand.
- Emails are detailed, formatted, and mistake-free.

- They rarely make instant decisions without researching first.

- They value documentation such as reports, case studies, timelines, data, and reviews.

- You'll spot a blue when they ask, "What's the error margin on this?" or, "Have you done a pilot rollout of this model before?" They're not trying to trip you up; they're testing the *system*. That's how their mind operates. They want to know if what you are proposing makes sense.

How to Sell to a Blue

Selling to a blue isn't about charm. It's about competence. They won't be wooed by enthusiasm or colourful slides. They want credibility.

Here's how you win them over:

- **Be prepared:** Don't wing it. Ever.

- **Show the full process:** Provide step-by-step timelines and deliverables.
- **Use data and case studies:** Show historical performance, outcomes, and metrics.

- **Don't overpromise:** If you don't know something, say so and get back to them.

Remember, a blue personality isn't trying to catch you out. They're trying to protect themselves, their team, and their reputation from chaos.

The Challenges with Blues

The blues can be judgmental. It's not that they mean to be. They have the highest expectations of other people for one simple reason, they also have the highest expectation of themselves. Blues can be overly analytical and may stall the deal with paralysis by analysis waiting for one more piece of information.

They may also be critical as they will spot inconsistencies, grammar issues, or weak logic instantly. They may also be emotionally reserved and may not give you affirmations, smiles or clear signals.

Blues get a dopamine hit not from fun or applause, but from **order**. From a spreadsheet that balances, a plan that anticipates risk, or a presentation that doesn't just inspire, but informs. They don't just want to win. They want to win correctly. This can be frustrating for a high-energy salesperson. You might think, "Am I losing them?" when in fact, they're just processing.

Useful Belief for Working with Blues

"They're not being difficult, they're being diligent. If I meet their need for clarity and structure, I can gain their respect and loyalty."

They'll ask about compliance, auditability, and version control. Not because they doubt you, but because they trust systems, not slogans. Follow up with a blue personality with a well-written summary. Include attachments, reference material, set expectations clearly, and offer to clarify any misunderstandings.

Blues will respect your professionalism, but only if it's authentic. Blues take longer to close, but when they do, they stay. Why? Because their decision-making process already accounted for the long game.

Questions to Ask Yourself

- Who are the blues in your life and business?

- Do you prepare with enough detail in your presentations to win their trust?

- How can you speak their language of process without losing your own voice?

- Selling to blue personalities isn't about spark or sizzle, but rather it's about substance. It's not about momentum, but rather method. Their loyalty is earned, not assumed. Their standards are high, but their respect is real. So, if you're willing to do the work to clarify, prepare, and prove, you'll not just make a sale, but also a true partnership.

COLOUR COMBINATIONS

Now that we've explored the four core personality colours of red, yellow, aqua, and blue, you're likely thinking, *I'm not just one colour! Don't box me in one colour!* And you would be right. It's time to talk about colour combinations.

While some people are just *red* all the time, or just *yellow* living in the moment, or just *aqua* and even-tempered, or just *blue* constantly needing things to make sense, many people are more than one colour. They're a mix.

You might be red in the boardroom but aqua when parenting. You might be yellow at a wedding but blue when planning your finances. You might lead with one colour in your career, and another in your closest relationships. That's the magic of human behaviour, and understanding these combinations is where true influence begins.

Because let's face it: no one is one-dimensional. People are dynamic. And when you learn how to spot the blends, not just the base tones, you move from good communicator to someone who *gets people*.

Let's break down some of the most common colour combinations you'll meet and how to work with them like a communication master.

Red-Yellow: The Energetic Achiever

Let's start with one close to home for me. I'm a red-yellow. That means I'm one of the easiest people in the world to sell to. Show me how it's going to get a result (red), make it fun or exciting (yellow), and throw in a compliment or two, and I'm there.

Red-yellow personalities are fast, loud, passionate, and results-driven. They move quickly, speak with conviction, and bring infectious energy to teams and projects. They're the sales directors who fire up a room. They're the entrepreneurs who launch the new idea before the ink is dry. They're the coaches, leaders, and influencers. The downside is they can burn bright and burn out. They can miss details, get distracted, and lose focus. They're allergic to routine, and often resist structure unless it's built for momentum.

☼ **Tip:** With red-yellow people, keep it punchy, positive, and action-oriented. Don't bog them down with spreadsheets. Show them what's possible and let them lead the charge.

Red-Blue: The Powerful Perfectionist

The powerful red-blue combo. I call this the multimillionaire's curve. These are the people who want to win and follow a process to do it. They're driven, disciplined, and determined to succeed on their own terms.

This personality type is common in elite athletes, high-level professionals, engineers, architects, and financial leaders. They combine the red's hunger for results with the blue's need for structure and excellence. They don't just want to grow the business; they want to scale it, refine it, and bulletproof it. They can be hard on themselves and others. And when stress hits, that pressure to perform perfectly can lead to overwork or criticism.

☼ **Tip:** Red-blue clients need to see how the process will directly lead to results. Make sure you have your presentation polished and you're prepared for the objections.

Yellow-Blue: The Creative Strategist

Yellow-blue is one of the most fascinating colour combos in any room. These personalities have the spark of creativity and the discipline of detail. They can brainstorm the next big idea and then build the system to deliver it.

These people are often top-tier marketers, project managers, brand strategists, or designers. They bring flair *and* form. The yellow in them thrives on possibility. The blue in them thrives on practicality. But internally? It can feel like a tug of war. One part wants to run with an idea. The other part wants to map out the risks. It's imagination meeting an Excel spreadsheet.

☀ **Tip:** When working with yellow-blues, fuel their excitement, but also respect their systems. Show how your offer or message checks *both* boxes: creative vision and logical delivery.

Blue-Aqua: The Quiet Trusted Professional

If there's a combination you want in your corner, it's this one. Blue-aquas are your kind, consistent, thoughtful professionals. They bring warmth and wisdom to everything they do.

These are the teachers, the administrators, the HR managers, the counsellors. They might not speak often in meetings, but when they do, everyone listens. They're often the moral compass of the room. They value integrity, loyalty, and service. They don't need the credit. They just want to make sure things are done properly.

☀ **Tip:** Blue-aqua personalities need both clarity and care. Communicate clearly. Deliver consistently. But also check in emotionally. A simple, "How are you feeling about this?" goes a long way.

Aqua-Yellow: The Heart of the Team

Aqua-yellows are gentle, warm, bubbly, and inclusive.

They care about how people feel and want everyone to have a good time along the way.

They're natural team players. They throw surprise birthdays, organise office trivia nights, and know how to make people laugh and feel included. They're the connectors who bring energy *and* empathy. They can struggle with boundaries. They may say yes to too much or ghost you because they hate saying no.

☼ **Tip:** Help aqua-yellows stay on track with gentle guidance. Encourage them to prioritise, but make it fun. Light reminders. Positive structure. Always with kindness.

CREATE HIGHER-LEVEL CONNECTION

When it comes to influence, there's no 'one-size-fits-all'. Understanding colour personalities and behavioural cues helps you meet people where they are. Adaptation isn't manipulation, but rather it's connection at a higher level. Customizing communication styles for deeper resonance and faster influence is just smart.

PART
FIVE

STRATEGIC CURIOSITY

◎ THE ART OF ASKING GREAT QUESTIONS

In every sales conversation, there's a secret advantage hiding in plain sight. It's not how well you present. It's not how sharp your slides are. It's how curious you are. True sales mastery isn't about overpowering your client with an impressive presentation. It's about creating a space where they feel safe enough to share what really matters. And you do that not by talking more, but rather by asking better questions.

The best salespeople in the world aren't the ones who dominate the conversation. They're the ones who strategically guide it. Strategic curiosity is about intentionally using questions to build trust, gather rich information, guide the client toward your solution, strengthen emotional connection, and ultimately win more business. It's not random curiosity. It's not interrogation. It's not a checklist of questions fired off in a robotic tone. It's strategic. Purposeful. Intentional. And when done right, it's an absolute game changer.

Most salespeople, unfortunately, fall into one of two traps. Some talk too much, believing that sheer enthusiasm will win the day. Others fire off surface-level questions like, "What's your budget?" or, "When are you looking to move forward?" without ever really understanding what the client cares about. Both approaches fail for the same reason: they miss the emotional engine of decision-making.

Psychology shows us that people don't make decisions based purely on logic. In his ground-breaking book *Thinking, Fast and Slow*, Nobel Prize winner Daniel Kahneman demonstrated that most decisions are made emotionally and then justified logically *after* the fact.[10]

When salespeople only play to logic, or worse, never even reach emotional engagement, they leave massive influence on the table.

When you ask the right questions, like the kind that move from surface to depth, you activate parts of the brain associated with emotional processing and relational trust. Neuroscience shows that when people feel truly listened to, their brains release oxytocin, a hormone that fosters trust and connection.[11] When you listen well and guide with curiosity, you're literally creating a neurochemical advantage in the conversation.

There's another reason strategic curiosity matters: it fights against one of the biggest hidden enemies in sales, which is assumption. The brain craves shortcuts. This is great for survival, but terrible for discovery. When we assume we know what the client wants, we stop listening. We stop being curious. We rush to solutions that don't fully match the real need. Then we wonder why deals fall apart or clients go cold.

Strategic curiosity keeps you in discovery mode longer. It slows you down. Because when you take the time to fully understand, you can tailor your offer so precisely it feels inevitable to the client.

Most importantly, strategic curiosity creates emotional investment. People value what they articulate themselves more than anything you say. If you help a client express their frustrations, dreams, and priorities, they feel ownership over the solution. They feel heard, and people who feel heard are far more likely to move forward with you.

So as we move into the practical framework of mastering the sales meeting, remember it's not about sounding impressive. It's not about controlling the conversation. It's about guiding it with intention, respect, and curiosity.

Because when you build conversations on a foundation of strategic curiosity, you're not just closing deals. You're opening relationships. You're earning influence. And you're creating opportunities that your competition will never even see.

Now let's dive into the framework that will help you lead every sales meeting with precision, power, and purpose.

THE STRATEGIC QUESTION LADDER

Top salespeople don't wing it in the discovery phase. They don't stumble into information, but rather elicit it purposefully, with precision and flow. One of the most powerful ways to do this is by using a structured framework called the Strategic Question Ladder.

The Strategic Question Ladder isn't just a series of random questions. It's a deliberate sequence that mirrors the way humans naturally reveal deeper truths. By climbing the ladder step-by-step, you create safety, build emotional momentum, and lead the client toward clarity, both for them and for you.

Let's walk through each of the five types of questions, or five steps on the ladder, for gathering the information you need to make the sale. They're logical and follow the process of what's happening for the customer. The ladder goes up step-by-step, uncovering their present situation, the problem they're looking to solve, the consequence of inaction, the ideal solution, and the decision-making process around getting started.

Situation Questions (Present State)

The first step is establishing the present reality. You start by asking neutral observational questions such as:

- "What's the current situation?"

- "Let's start by talking about what's happening now. Can you tell me about the current process?"

- "Before we talk about some of the challenges you're facing, tell me a little bit about what's working well at the moment?"

- "How are your people feeling right now about the current system?"

- These questions serve two purposes: they allow the client to speak comfortably about familiar territory, and they give you critical context. You're not just gathering facts; you're also calibrating their language, energy, and priorities.

▥ Challenge Questions (What Problem Are We Solving?)

Once the client feels comfortable, now it's time to take the next step on the ladder and gently guide them into uncovering challenges. These questions may include:

- "Tell me what the challenges are at the moment?"

- "What needs to happen for you to get what you want?

- "Where is the system falling down?"

- "What's the next step in the process for you? What do you need to do to get there?"

These questions are about uncovering real needs. Acknowledging their frustrations respectfully builds rapport and positions you as a problem-solver, not a product-pusher.

▥ Impact Questions (Why It Matters)

Impact questions are the next step up, and they dig

even deeper. Here, you're helping the client connect their challenges to consequences. You move from surface problems to emotional stakes. This is where real urgency is born. These questions may include:

- "What's the consequence if you don't make a change soon?"

- "What will happen to the organisation if you don't get this fixed?"

- "What's the impact on the people if this system remains the same?"

- "How will you feel in twelve months if you haven't taken action on this?"

- Neurologically, this taps into the brain's limbic system, which is the emotional centre that drives decisions. People act when they feel the cost of inaction, not just when they intellectually understand it. What's the consequence if they do nothing?

Desire Questions (Ideal Future)

After exploring the potential consequences of not acting, the next step up the ladder pivots to hope. These questions help the customer paint a vivid positive vision of the future. This is called 'future pacing', a powerful technique from neurolinguistic programming that makes desired outcomes feel real and attainable.

- "If everything worked out perfectly, what would it look like?"

- "What would success feel like for you?"

- "For you to tell others that was a great selling experience, what would have happened?"

- "Six months from now, when this is all over, what do you want your situation to be?"

- Creating this emotional contrast, moving from current pain to future pleasure, magnifies motivation for the customer to act.

Decision Questions (How Decisions Get Made)

Finally, at the top of the ladder, it's time to address the buying mechanics. These questions give clarity on the ideal timeline the client wants to get started. Without asking these questions, you risk building all the emotional momentum up for the sale, only to crash into logistical barriers later.

- "Who, apart from yourselves, are involved in making this decision?"

- "What is your timeline? When will you ideally be ready to get started?"

- "What has to be finished before we can start the project?"

- "For us to be finished by the end of the year, will you be ready to start next week?"

Asking about the decision-making process signals professionalism and foresight. Even more importantly, it incites action, as it also activates Dr. Robert Cialdini's psychological principle of 'commitment and consistency', which states that once people articulate their decision process, they're more likely to follow through.

Bringing It All Together

Structuring your questions isn't about being robotic. It's about orchestrating a conversation that feels natural yet purposeful. One mistake salespeople make is they don't follow a structure when asking questions. They just ask whatever pops into their mind. I challenge you to go through the questions you ask in a normal sales meeting and structure them to follow a process. By following a structure, you lead the customer on a journey that helps both of you gain clarity about what must be achieved and which problems must be solved.

When you climb the Strategic Question Ladder correctly:

- Clients feel heard and understood.

- You uncover not just the needs of the customer, but also the drivers behind the decision-making.

- You position yourself not just as a salesperson, but as a trusted guide.

THE 1%ERS OF STRATEGIC CURIOSITY

While you're climbing the Strategic Question Ladder, there are a number of mindset and language tools that will help you control the conversion and also elicit more valuable information. I call this series of tools the 1%ers, and you can use them throughout the discovery process.

Let's start with making sure you're clear about your outcome and what you want to achieve before you ever start asking questions and heading up that powerful Strategic Question Ladder.

MINDSET TOOL: KNOW YOUR OUTCOME

Before you walk into any meeting, virtual platform, or even pick up the phone, you need one thing: a clear outcome. It sounds simple. Yet this one habit is the invisible divider between average salespeople and those who consistently dominate their field.

> *"If you aim at nothing, you*
> *will hit it every time."*
> *– Zig Ziglar*

Without a clearly defined outcome, a meeting becomes a meandering conversation – a coffee chat with no direction. You may build rapport; you may even enjoy yourself, but you'll most likely leave without a win. A meeting with no outcome is a missed opportunity to move a relationship, a deal, or a decision forward.

The danger is that without realizing it, you begin to normalise 'good conversations' that go nowhere. You leave too much to chance. You hand the steering wheel of the meeting to the client, who has no obligation to drive it toward your goals. It's your responsibility to lead, not through pressure, but through clarity. Clear intention doesn't mean aggressive selling. It means knowing where you want to go and quietly and confidently guiding the conversation there.

Knowing your outcome also protects you against one of the great invisible killers in sales: cognitive overload. Otherwise known as going down the rabbit hole. Without a clear objective, it's easy to get swept into every tangent the client offers and chase interesting but irrelevant topics, trying to solve every problem at once. A clear outcome keeps you anchored. It lets you steer the conversation gently back when it drifts. It gives you permission to say, "That's a great point, and I'd love to circle back to it. But first can we dig a little deeper into your priority?"

Before you go to the meeting, know your outcome. When you have clarity about your outcome, you project calmness. There's no frantic grasping for the next thing to say. No desperate improvisation. You're simply moving from point A to point B with quiet certainty. Clients feel that. People buy from those who seem to know where they're going, not just with the sale, but with the relationship.

Ask yourself:

- What's my ideal outcome for this conversation?
- What would a win look like?
- What do I want the next steps to be following this meeting?

Your outcome might be:

- Booking that next meeting.
- Discovering who the decision makers actually are.
- Uncovering the real need under the surface.
- Understanding the customer buying timeline.
- Earning permission to submit a proposal.
- Making a sale.

The outcome isn't always about closing the sale on the spot, but rather creating progress.

LANGUAGE TOOL: THE MOMENT OF TRUTH AND A POLITE BEGINNING

Every great sales meeting has a moment that shifts from small talk to business. It's that subtle shift when the pleasantries fade, the jokes settle, the coffee cools, and the client, whether explicitly or silently, signals that they're ready to get down to business. This may be signalled with the customer asking, "Alright, what have you got for me?" Or it may be more subtle than that. The customer may glance at their phone or their watch, possibly shift in their seat. Either way, you notice it. You can feel it. It's time to get down to business.

This is the *moment of truth*, and in this moment, it's time to take control of the sales meeting.

Many salespeople miss this moment entirely. They ride the wave of early rapport a little too long, lose the client's attention, and suddenly find themselves chasing the conversation instead of leading it. Or they jump into their presentation, abruptly shifting gears and jarring the emotional flow they had built. Both mistakes are costly and can derail a perfectly good opportunity.

Mastering the moment of truth is about seizing leadership of the meeting, but doing it with grace, not force. It's about setting the stage, so the client feels respected, not railroaded. It's about creating a natural bridge from casual connection to purposeful conversation. And that bridge is built with one key tool: a polite beginning.

Polite beginning is a three-step conversational move that elegantly transitions you into the 'business' portion of the meeting. It involves thanking the client, stating your outcome, and asking permission to ask questions. Simple? Yes. But also profound.

Three-Step Polite Beginning

- **Thank Them**

  "First of all, thank you for the opportunity to meet with you today."

- **State Your Outcome**

  "My outcome today is really to understand what's most important to you and share a little about how we might be able to help."

- **Ask Permission to Ask Questions**

  "To make sure I understand that properly, would it be OK if I asked you a few questions?"

It's just a polite way to start. Even better, the answer to the question will almost certainly be a yes. In fact, you may even see the customer relax, sit back, and get ready for you to go into the discovery phase, asking the questions from the strategic question ladder.

In a world where most salespeople are still guessing their way through the discovery phase, mastering this structure will set you up to succeed. Influence doesn't happen by accident. It happens by design.

LANGUAGE TOOL: MOVE TO THE SIDE

This is one of my favourite language tools. There's a mistake many salespeople make during the discovery phase: they make assumptions. They often assume the first answer as the *real* answer. For example, if you ask a client, "What's important to you in this process?" it's possible the response you receive from the customer will be money-related such as "Price," "Best deal," or "Lowest cost." It's almost automatic for customers to respond this way because they don't want to get taken advantage of. And while these answers from the customer are easy, they're rarely the full truth.

If you anchor your entire presentation around that first response, you're stuck playing a commodity game. You're negotiating on price, trapped in a race to the bottom, instead of selling based on value, trust, and transformation.

That's why I love the language tool 'move to the side'.

When a client says "Price," it's not about challenging them. Instead, it's important to validate the importance of price, and then gently move past it. It might sound something like, "Most people usually answer the same way. People want to talk about price, and, of course, that's hugely important. We'll absolutely talk about that and make sure you're comfortable with everything to do with that. But just putting price **to the side** for a moment, aside from price, what's the most important thing for you in this process to get the outcome you need?"

In that moment, the client reflects and considers the aspects of the process aside from money, and in the next few moments, you'll uncover their real buying motives. The answers could be any number of things, including:

- Communication

- Transparency

- Trust

- Relationship

- Technology platform

- Ongoing service

The 'move to the side' tool helps you get money out of the way in the short term to discover what will really give value to the client, depending on the industry or service.

LANGUAGE TOOL: HOW DO YOU MEAN?

Following on from the last language tool where we moved price to the side, the answers from the customer were things like communication, transparency, trust, relationship, technology platform, ongoing service, and possibly hundreds of others. Here's where you can get caught by assuming you know what they mean by those answers. For example, if *communication* is the answer, do I really know what that means? Really? Or am I making assumptions? Do they want to be able to access the progress of the project 24 hours a day? Or do they want me to call them once a month? I don't really know. Therefore, this simple question will give you all the information you need. "**How** do you mean?"

This is one of the most underrated, powerful, and frankly enjoyable tools you can use in a sales conversation. It might seem small, almost casual, possibly grammatically incorrect, but when this language tool is deployed correctly, it gives you a flood of information that can give you a greater understanding of your customer.

How does this work?

First, it's important to notice it's "*how* do you mean?" and not "*what* do you mean?" There's a subtle but critical difference. When you ask, "What do you mean?" it can sometimes imply that the client was unclear or you didn't understand them properly. It can create a tiny ripple of defensiveness, even if unintended. "*How* do you mean?" is softer, more curious, more collaborative. It signals: "I'm interested. I want to understand more deeply. Help me understand."

With this tool, the delivery matters just as much as the words. I always recommend asking "how do you mean?" with a genuine tone of curiosity, maybe even a slight tilt of the head and in a slightly higher-pitched tone of voice. Possible even with a slight stutter.

"When you say communication is the most important thing, h-h-how do you mean?"

Now you begin to get a flood of information. The customer replies with, "Well, I suppose, for us, good communication would be really important because …" They keep talking and give you tremendous insight into what's important about communication.

Why's this so powerful? Because when customers talk about 'trust', 'support', 'partnership', or 'results' it sounds great, but they're incredibly broad ideas. Different customers mean different things because they interpret ideas differently based on their experiences, expectations, and even fears. If you don't seek clarification, you risk selling to the wrong idea.

For example, a client might say, "Trust is really important to me." If you assume you know what they mean, you might start talking about detailed contracts and transparency reports. But if you pause and ask, "H-h-how do you mean?" they might reveal, "Well, I'm too busy to micromanage this project – I need to know I can leave it with you, and it'll be done." Completely different. Now you know exactly how to frame your solution.

In addition, when clients explain their meaning in their own words, they're reinforcing their own buying motives. Remember, customers are more likely to act when *they* have articulated what they want.

LANGUAGE TOOL: TRANSFER THE TALKING STICK

There comes a moment in every great sales conversation when the discovery phase comes to an end and it's time to move out of strategic curiosity – which means it's time for you to shine. It's time for you to deliver your sales presentation and demonstrate 'why you?' While hopefully the client has been doing most of the talking throughout the discovery phase, it's now time to take the talking stick because you're ready to deliver the solution your company offers.

You've built rapport and asked the right questions; you've listened, peeled back the layers, uncovered the client's real needs, and made them feel seen, heard, and valued. Now it's time to pivot. It's time to move from discovery into presentation, from questions into solutions, and here's the tool to transfer you into that space.

Transfer the Talking Stick

You can't just bulldoze and start selling. There's an artful respectful move, an elegant passing of the conversation baton. Of course, you can't just grab the talking stick. You must be handed the stick by the customer. The art form is creating a clean permission-based transition that feels natural.

It may sound like this: "Thank you so much for sharing all of that with me. It really gives me a clear picture of what is important to you and the problem we're here to solve. If it's alright with you, I'd love to take the next few minutes and walk you through how we can help."

When done well, the customer answers, "Sounds good" and leans back in their chair in listening mode. You've done it. They've been heard, and now they're ready to hear. This is your time to shine.

Obviously, you'll say this in *your* style of speaking and language. It may be: "I really appreciate you taking the time to walk me through everything that's important to you. Would it be OK if I shared some ideas about how we could support what you're trying to achieve?"

Or …

"It sounds like there are three major things you're trying to solve. A, B, and C. If you're open to it, I'd love to walk you through how I know we could help."

This gives you structure. So many salespeople get lost in what I call the 'land of the unknown tongue' where they're just talking, selling a little, asking some questions, going down an irrelevant rabbit hole, then selling some more, and finally trying a close. Instead, this is a process. This is a structure. When you're ready to move out of the discovery phase and into the presentation phase, this tool will make that transition seamless.

Here's another bonus. When you transfer the talking stick properly, your presentation becomes 10 times easier. Why? You're not presenting into a defensive mind. Instead, you're presenting to an open mind that's already primed to listen because they've given you permission to lead them.

MASTERING THE 1%ERS OF STRATEGIC CURIOSITY

In the fast-moving world of sales, it's easy for conversations to spiral. A client asks a question, you answer. Another question pops up, you chase it. Before you know it, the meeting has become a loose, meandering dialogue with no real direction and no clear outcome. Salespeople who drift through meetings without a process tend to lose control, and when you lose control, you usually lose the business. That's why this structure matters so much. It's the structure that transforms a conversation from chaos into clarity, from random dialogue into purposeful movement toward a decision.

The 1%ers of strategic curiosity include:

- Know your outcome before you show up.

- Recognise that the moment of truth has happened, the small talk is over, and the meeting is moving to the business phase.
- Master the three-step polite beginning to put the customer at ease and get them ready to answer questions.

- Move to the side discussions of money, price, and fee to discover what's truly important to the customer in the selling process.

- Dig deeper with, "H-h-how do you mean?" get a flood of information, and gain a greater understanding of your customer.

- Once all the questions have been asked, transfer the talking stick, put them in listening mode, and get ready to present your solution.

- Mastering strategic curiosity only works when you're truly prepared to listen more than you speak. Listening isn't passive, but rather it's a deliberate act of validation.

When clients feel genuinely heard, you earn the ultimate currency in sales – trust.

Salespeople who master these tools of strategic curiosity don't just run better meetings; they create better outcomes. They maintain flow and control without ever feeling aggressive or manipulative. They become trusted advisors rather than salespeople chasing deals.

Control isn't about dominance. It's about direction. By following this structured path, you stay in the driver's seat, leading conversations with confidence, clarity, and influence all the way to a successful outcome.

PART
SIX

WIN THE SHORT GAME AND THE LONG GAME

◎ CLOSING THE SALE AND BUILDING THE RELATIONSHIP

Here we are near the end. You've built rapport. You've asked the right questions, listened with intention, and delivered a presentation that aligned with the client's deepest needs and desires. You've done all the heavy lifting. Now comes the moment that many salespeople fear: the close. The word itself often carries tension. Closing can feel final, heavy, even aggressive, conjuring images of pressure tactics and desperate last-ditch efforts. But when you're succeeding at the highest level, that image couldn't be further from the truth.

Closing isn't about slamming the door shut. It isn't about trapping a client in a decision they're not ready for. True closing is about guiding the next step, whatever that next step looks like. It's about momentum, not manipulation. It's about trust, not tricks. It's about moving the relationship forward, whether that movement is a signed contract today or simply a stronger bridge toward tomorrow.

The truth is sometimes you close the sale today and other times you simply help the client move one step closer to saying yes. Both are wins.

SHORT GAME MINDSET – CLOSING THE BUSINESS TODAY

A strong close is about maintaining the energy, curiosity, and enthusiasm you built throughout the meeting. It's not a dramatic ending, but rather it's a transition, and every interaction, every micro-decision along the way contributes to that momentum.

Imagine a great conversation with a friend. You don't rush them to a decision. You don't badger them into agreeing with you. Instead, you create an environment where it's easy and natural for them to move closer to your point of view. That's how closing should feel. Warm.

Connected. Forward-moving.

In psychological terms, this once again leverages the principle of commitment and consistency founded by Dr. Robert Cialdini in his work on influence. When people take small voluntary steps toward a decision, they're more likely to follow through with larger commitments later. If you've guided your client through a series of micro-yeses where they've been agreeing with your questions, nodding to the pain points, and envisioning their future success, the final decision feels like the obvious natural outcome.

However, if you've skipped those steps and made it all about your product, your presentation, and your need to close the sale, the final ask feels jarring. Even if your solution is brilliant, the lack of emotional and psychological preparation creates friction.

The reality is simple: every sales conversation eventually comes to a fork in the road. One path leads to indecision, delay, or disengagement. The other leads to a decision and, ideally, to a new client relationship. The professional's job is to guide the client toward that decision point with skill, not force, making this a natural transition.

The best way to make that transition? The 'trial close question'.

THE TRIAL CLOSE QUESTION AND NAVIGATING OBJECTIONS

After you've presented your solution and hopefully aligned it beautifully with the customer's needs, you don't just sit back and hope they'll magically announce they're ready to proceed. You also don't want to fill the space with nervous rambling, overwhelming them with more features and benefits they didn't ask for. Instead, you lean in with a simple trial close question.

"Based on everything we've discussed, what are your thoughts?"

That's it. Clean. Respectful. Nonthreatening. Inviting. It hands the client the emotional space to respond without feeling cornered. It respects their autonomy and opens a safe pathway for them to share where they're at.

Once you ask your trial close question, you'll typically hear one of two positive responses. Each one signals a different pathway for your next move. The responses could be:

"Sounds good!" 🎯

This is the dream response. The energy is aligned. The trust is there. They're ready to move forward. Internally, you can celebrate, but externally, stay calm and professional. Smoothly guide them through the next steps.

"Sounds good, but ..."

The customer is almost there. They may just be working through one or two final friction points. They may say, "Sounds good, but it's too expensive." This is where you can work a simple four-part process called *navigating objections.* This process includes clarifying the objection, making a statement that lets them know you understand them, isolating that objection to the side to discover if there are further objections, and then finally answering the objection. Let's go through these four steps and how this would work.

INFLUENCE TOOL: NAVIGATING OBJECTIONS

Step 1: Clarify the Objection

First, you need to truly understand what 'too expensive' means. You don't really know. Therefore, it's important to clarify in which context it's too expensive. It may sound like this: "When you say it's too expensive, h-h-how do you mean? Is that compared to the budget or compared to your expectation? Tell me a little bit about that."

Step 2: Deliver a Pace Statement

Once they tell you more specifics and you have more information, one of the most powerful things you can do is what I call a 'pace statement'. This is simply a statement to the customer that lets them know you appreciate where they're coming from and you're on the same side. You can start it with the words, "It's pretty important …" and finish with a question, "… isn't it?" It might sound like this: "It's pretty important at the end of the day that you feel like you got value for money, isn't it?" They'll say yes, and you're seen as appreciating where they're coming from.

Step 3: Move to the Side

Now that they recognise you're listening to them, it's important to isolate the objection to determine if anything else is holding you back. We can bring back 'move to the side' and find out if this is the only objection we must work through. It may be: "Great. Well, just taking the price and moving it to the side for a moment, aside from the price, is there anything else holding us back today from moving forward?"

Step 4: Answer the Objection

Now if there's nothing else, we can simply enter a negotiation on price. Before doing so, I do want to double-check that I have commitment. "Just to confirm, if we can agree on price, are you happy to move forward?

Great. Let's see if we can make this work." You can now negotiate to see if you're able to reach an agreement. If there is another objection, you can follow the same four-step process to clarify, pace, and isolate it, and then answer both objections.

When you handle this moment well, you can win the business and strengthen the relationship. The client now needs to see you not just as a salesperson, but as a partner in solving problems.

It's your job to stay curious, not defensive.

Objections aren't rejections. They're just unanswered questions in the client's mind.

INFLUENCE TOOL: POSITIVE, POSITIVE, POSITIVE, NEGATIVE

One tool that may help at the end of answering the objection and help the customer act is positive, positive, positive, negative. In the world of influence and closing, there are few techniques as simple, natural, and psychologically powerful as this one. It's a method that doesn't just close someone, but rather guides them, using the universal drivers of human decision-making: the pursuit of pleasure and the avoidance of pain.

This concept draws heavily from classic psychology, particularly Sigmund Freud's pain-pleasure principle and later Daniel Kahneman's and Amos Tversky's ground-breaking work on loss aversion. Their research showed that human beings are *twice as motivated to avoid pain* than to seek pleasure.[12] In other words, people act faster to avoid a loss than to secure a gain.

When you understand this, positive, positive, positive, negative becomes a master key to decision-making influence. It gives your client a clear emotional reason to move forward, not just based on what they stand to gain, but on what they stand to lose if they hesitate.

The Positive, Positive, Positive, Negative Structure

- State three positives. Anchor the person in all the things they desire and are right about the decision they're about to make.

- Then gently introduce a negative and highlight what they risk losing if they don't act, using the powerful words, "What would be a shame …"

To make this come alive, I'll use a real estate sales example with an agent and a buyer who has spent a long time looking for a home and hasn't decided yet. In this scenario, the house is exactly what they've said they're after.

- "You've been looking for months, and this house has the dream kitchen, which was at the top of your list, that you love." **Positive.**

- "It has the four-bedroom accommodation you require, plus the study upstairs." **Positive.**
- "Also, it's just a five-minute walk from the school. Close, but not too close when it gets busy at drop-off and pickup times." **Positive.**

- "Mr. and Mrs. Jones, **what would be a shame** is if we don't move on this tonight and by the end of Saturday's open house someone else wants in on the bidding and you end up paying $30,000 more. You have an opportunity here. Let's do this thing." **Negative.**

Positive, positive, positive, negative balances both motivational levers. It builds emotional attachment to the positives and creates a healthy urgency through potential loss. Every decision we make carries both gain and risk. You're just making both sides visible. You can also use this tool in everyday life. Here's a mom trying to get her daughter to clean her room before going to the park:

- "Hey, Savannah, I just got off the phone with Coco's mum. We're going to the park (positive), having a big picnic (positive), and then going to the movies together (positive)."

- "Now, Savannah, what would be a shame is if you didn't clean your room, and we had to cancel this fun day we're going to have (negative)."
Here's another example in recruitment:

- "You've got the skills we need (positive). Your experience fits in perfectly with where we want to go as a company (positive). Maybe most importantly, your values really fit our culture here (positive).

- "What would be a shame is if you missed this opportunity because you waited too long to make this decision (negative)."

You get the idea. It's important to know that this tool is about *authentic guidance*, not fearmongering. You're not creating artificial fear. You're simply being real about the consequences of inaction. If you exaggerate or manipulate, people will feel it, and you'll break trust. But when you genuinely care and when you believe your client will be better off acting now, this technique becomes a service, not a tactic. You're helping them see the whole chessboard.

LONG GAME MINDSET – BUILDING CLIENTS FOR LIFE

There's a certain magic in sales that isn't found in quick wins or flashy closes. It's found in the patient consistent art of building relationships that last. In a world obsessed with instant gratification, mastering the long game isn't just a competitive advantage, but rather it's a calling card of true professionals.

Sometimes, despite your best efforts, you won't close the deal today. Sometimes it's a big-ticket program that will take multiple meetings to close. Sometimes there are multiple decision-makers, and the process of getting a project off the ground will take many months. Sometimes it's as simple as the timing isn't quite right, and the salesperson has to be patient.

The key to winning the long game is to always be moving to the next steps. For each meeting, you can follow the processes in this book to get the big deal over the line. So what are some of the keys to winning the patient sale?:

- **Follow up thoughtfully**: Stay in touch in a way that shows you're aware of the problem they need to solve and thinking of them, without asking for anything directly in return.

- **Stay visible**: Out of sight, out of mind. Stay aware of wins and recent successes for the customer. This may also mean commenting on and sharing social media insights.

- **Continually add value**: This could be sharing an idea they hadn't considered, offering to introduce them to a contact, or sending them early access to something useful such as a white paper or webinar.

Every time you show up with value, without a sales pitch attached, you deepen the relationship and increase the chances of the successful long game sale. One of the most important elements of the long game is respecting the client's timeline. If you try to force a timeline, you erode trust. Let the client know they'll have your full support when they're ready.

Each contact could be a small nudge. You don't need to make massive leaps every time. The question is always about progress. With every contact, did you move the relationship forward today?

In summary, some deals close today. Some other seeds take years to bear fruit. Sales mastery demands both urgency and patience. It's knowing when to close with strength, and when to invest in long-term trust. Sales is about balancing immediate results with lifetime client relationship building.

PART
SEVEN

SUNSET GOAL SETTING

◎ DESIGNING A LIFE OF EXCELLENCE

In the quiet golden hours of the evening, as the sun dips below the horizon, we're offered one of life's simplest and greatest moments: the sunset. A sunset is nature's gentle reminder that every day, every chapter, and every season has an ending. It asks nothing from us except reflection and perhaps a small internal vow that tomorrow we'll be more awake, more intentional, and more alive.

In business and in life, the same principle applies. Seasons end. Chapters close. Days slip away. The question isn't whether time will pass, because it most certainly will. The question is whether we will live deliberately within it. Do we shape our journey with purpose, or are we simply passengers? This is the heart of *sunset goal setting*:

designing life and business with intention.

For many salespeople, the tragedy isn't that they lack talent. It's that they drift. They stay busy without ever getting results. They confuse motion for progress. In a world saturated with distractions, the art of setting meaningful goals and living toward them with focus has never been more essential.

Sunset goal setting isn't about making longer to-do lists. It's about building a life and business you're proud of. It's about anchoring yourself to sunsets, not vague hopes but specific powerful seasons of commitment and action.

SUNSET AS A METAPHOR

Let's talk about the future. The great thing is you can create a 'perfect world scenario' into the future. The sunset is a tool that can help you master your timeline and gain great clarity about what you want to achieve.

Let's do an exercise. I'm going to take you time travelling into the future. Imagine three months from now you ring your best friend, and you say, "I've never been happier in my job than I am right now. I've never been more fulfilled in my business than I am right now."

What would it take for you to say these words? What would have to happen between now and then? What did you do? What did you put in place? The answer is the action you need to take. This is your 90-day sunset.

Let's go forward 12 months from now. Walking into your sales conference having achieved your financial goal, what would that feel like? For you to reach that goal, what would have to happen between now and then? What did you do? What did you put in place? The answer is the action you need to take. This is your 12-month sunset.

When we think of goal setting, we often think in broad unfocused terms. "I want to be more successful." "I want to get healthier." "I want to grow my business." These are nice ideas, but without structure, they dissolve into wishful thinking.

Sunset goal setting changes the frame. It reminds you that life is lived in chapters. A sunset marks the end of a period, which could be 30, 60, 90, or 365 days. Or longer. It provides a natural closing, a line in the sand where we can reflect, recalibrate, and renew.

In today's business world full of distraction, clarity is more important than ever. Companies, leaders, and salespeople who fail to set clear goals can become victims of reactive living. They respond instead of creating. They survive instead of thriving.

THE SIX AREAS OF IMPORTANCE

In my experience working with thousands of salespeople, entrepreneurs, and leaders, fulfillment doesn't come from business success alone. It comes from balance across six key areas:

- **Family**: The foundation of belonging and identity.

- **Friends**: The community of chosen allies who fuel joy.

- **Health**: The vital engine without which nothing else runs.

- **Work**: The arena where contribution and creativity collide.

- **Community**: The channel for generosity and legacy.

- **Me time**: The often-forgotten realm of personal passion and reflection.

With each of the six areas of importance, sunset goal setting invites us to ask:

☐ What's your 30-day sunset goal?

☐ What's your 90-day sunset goal?

☐ What's your 365-day sunset goal?

One of the best ways to approach setting sunset goals is to perform an audit of action, asking yourself what you must do to achieve your goals in each area. What do you need to stop doing, start doing, and keep doing?

☐ START: What do I need to begin doing that aligns with the life I want to build?

☐ STOP: What habits, mindsets, or patterns are stealing energy and focus from my dreams?

☐ KEEP: What am I doing well that I must protect, nurture, and celebrate?

In business, particularly in sales, the danger of living without sunsets is motivation dips after every lost deal. Sales cycles drag indefinitely; pipeline management becomes guesswork, and momentum is replaced with frustration. Psychologically, this is called 'learned helplessness', which is a condition where repeated failures without clear feedback loops cause people to give up effort altogether. They believe they have no control, so they lose agency.

Sunsets restore agency. They put an end date on effort. They offer a finish line to sprint toward. Even if you don't win every race, you know when one race ends and another begins. Sunsets also create built-in small wins. You either cross the finish line, or you learn what needs to change before the next one.

HOW TO BUILD YOUR SUNSET

Goal setting without execution is just dreaming. Here's how you turn your sunsets into a living breathing reality:

1. Choose the Time Horizon
30, 60, 90, or 365 days. What feels right for this chapter in each of the six areas of importance?

2. Write Down Specific Goals
Vague is the enemy. *Get fitter* becomes, *Run 5 kilometres without stopping by September 1st.*

3. Create Emotional Anchors

Why does this goal matter to you? Who are you becoming by pursuing it?

4. Build Structures of Accountability

Deadlines. Check-ins. Mentors. Scoreboards. Systems beat willpower.

5. Celebrate the Sunset

Win or lose, when the sunset arrives, *pause*. Reflect. Celebrate growth.

Great sales careers don't happen by accident. Instead, they're designed with clarity and purpose. Sunset goal setting is about crafting goals that fuel meaning, focus, fulfillment, and legacy. When the sun sets on your career, what story will you have written?

Master the seven pillars of MindSell, and you won't just transform your sales … you'll transform your life.

ABOUT
THE AUTHOR

Chris Helder is a professional speaker and author known for his explosive energy, engaging style, humour, and delivering takeaways for clients that can be implemented immediately. He is a master in the areas of mindset, communication, and influence skills, and has been the keynote speaker at high-profile conferences around the world.

Chris is the author of seven books, including *MindSell: The Best Little Sales Book Ever, Re-Ignition: Finding Power When You Feel Flat, Tired and Uninspired*; and *The Ultimate Book of Influence: 10 Tools of Persuasion to Connect, Communicate, and Win in Business.* His best-selling book *Useful Belief: Because It's Better than Positive Thinking* is one of Australia's highest selling business books.

Chris has presented at over 2,500 conferences around the world, sharing his insights and strategies on how to communicate effectively, inspire and motivate teams, and achieve success in business and life.

He is known for his ability to connect with all types of audiences, using real-life examples and humour to drive his message home. His goal is to inspire individuals and organisations to think differently and achieve their full potential.

chrishelder.com.au

Audiobook

MindSell is also available in audio format.

Jump onto your favourite audiobook platform to have the story narrated for you by the author.

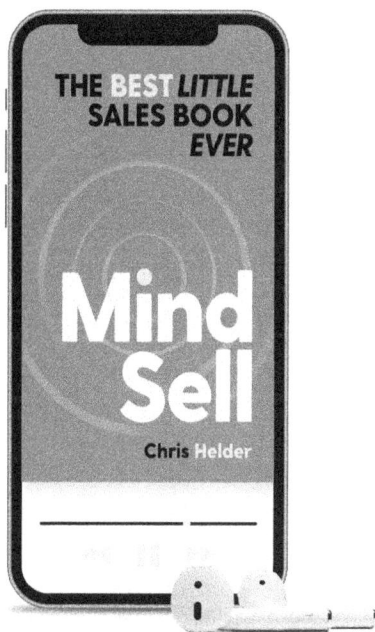

ENDNOTES

1   Gartner. n.d. "Buyer Enablement." Accessed June 3, 2025, https://www.gartner.com/en/sales/insights/buyer-enablement

2   Brooks, Alison Wood. 2013. "Get Excited: Reappraising Pre-Performance Anxiety as Excitement." *Journal of Experimental Psychology: General* 143, no. 3 (June): 1144–1158. doi.org/10.1037/a0035325.

3   Brooks, Alison Wood. 2013. "Get Excited: Reappraising Pre-Performance Anxiety as Excitement." *Journal of Experimental Psychology: General* 143, no. 3 (June): 1144–1158. doi.org/10.1037/a0035325.

4   Nowicki, Stephen, Yasmin Iles-Caven, Ari Kalechstein, and Jean Golding. 2021. "Editorial: Locus of Control: Antecedents, Consequences and Interventions Using Rotter's Definition." *Frontiers in Psychology* 12 (June). doi.org/10.3389/fpsyg.2021.698917.

5   Chand, Suma P., Daniel P. Kuckel, and Martin R. Huecker MR. 2023. "Cognitive Behavior Therapy." *StatPearls*. https://www.ncbi.nlm.nih.gov/books/NBK470241/

6   Center for Self-Determination Theory. n.d. "Theory." Accessed June 4, 2025. https://selfdeterminationtheory.org/theory/.

7   Mehrabian, Albert. n.d. "'Silent Messages' -- a Wealth of Information About Nonverbal Communication (Body Language)." *KAAJ*. Accessed June 4, 2025. https://www.kaaj.com/psych/smorder.html.

8   Gable, Shelly L., Harry T. Reis, Emily A. Impett, and Evan R. Asher. 2004. "What Do You Do When Things Go Right? The Intrapersonal and Interpersonal Benefits of Sharing Positive Events." *Journal of Personality and Social Psychology* 87, no. 2 (August): 228–245. doi.org/10.1037/0022-3514.87.2.228.

9   Cahill, Larry and James L. McGaugh. 1995. "A Novel Demonstration of Enhanced Memory Associated with Emotional Arousal." *Consciousness and Cognition* 4, no. 4 (December): 410–421. doi.org/10.1006/ccog.1995.1048.

10 Kahneman, Daniel. 2013. *Thinking, Fast and Slow*. New York City: Farrar, Straus and Giroux.

11 Harvard Health Publishing. n.d. "Oxytocin: The Love Hormone." *Harvard Medical School*. Accessed June 5, 2025. https://www.health.harvard.edu/mind-and-mood/oxytocin-the-love-hormone.

12 Harmon, Angela. 2025. "Loss Aversion." *EBSCO*. Accessed June 5, 2025. https://www.ebsco.com/research-starters/social-sciences-and-humanities/loss-aversion.